START-UP CITIZENSHIP

DIVERSE WORLD

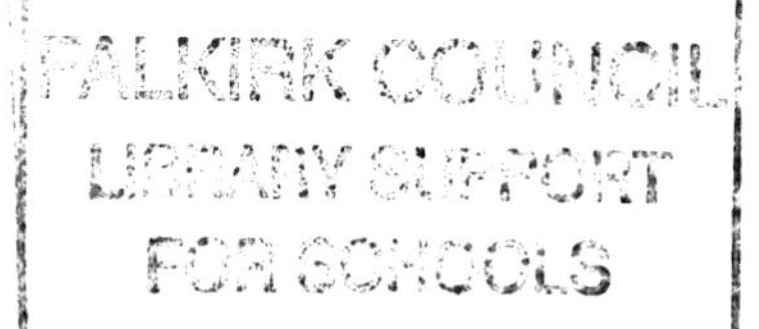

Louise and Richard Spilsbury

Published by Evans Brothers Limited
2A Portman Mansions
Chiltern Street
London W1U 6NR

Produced for Evans Brothers Limited by
White-Thomson Publishing Ltd.
Bridgewater Business Centre, 210 High Street,
Lewes, East Sussex BN7 2NH

Printed in China by WKT Co. Ltd.

Editor: Clare Collinson
Consultant: Roy Honeybone, Consultant in Citizenship Education and Editor of *Teaching Citizenship*, the journal of the Association for Citizenship Teaching
Designer: Leishman Design

British Library Cataloguing in Publication Data
Spilsbury, Louise
Diverse World. - (Start-up Citizenship)
1. Communities - Juvenile literature 2. Social networks - Juvenile literature 3. Intercultural communication - Juvenile literature 4. Citizenship - Juvenile literature
I. Title II. Spilsbury, Richard, 1963-
302.4

ISBN13: 9780237532666

Acknowledgements:
Special thanks to the following for their help and involvement with the preparation of this book: staff, pupils and parents at Holyoakes Field First School, Redditch, Mount Carmel RC First School, Redditch and St Stephen's CE First School, Redditch.

Picture Acknowledgements:
Alamy pp. 5t (Mitch Diamond), 14 (Sally and Richard Greenhill); Martyn Chillmaid pp. 4r, 6, 9, 12l, 19, 20; Corbis pp. 4l, 11l (Don Mason), 15 (Jose Luis Pelaez, Inc.), 16 (Roman Soumar), 17 (Roger De La Harpe; Gallo Images); Getty Images p. 10 (Ryan McVay); Roy Honeybone 21 (both); iStockphoto.com cover pp. 5b, title page and 11r; Topfoto p. 18 (Topham Picturepoint); WTPix pp. 7, 12r, 13 (both).

The map on page 8 was created by Peter Bull Art Studio, Ltd.

Contents

Who are you?

In our diverse world there are many different kinds of people. How are you different from other people?

"In my class I am the only person who can speak Chinese."

▶ **Your identity is what makes you special. How would you draw yourself in a self-portrait?**

diverse identity self-portrait

We are individuals but we all belong to different groups and communities. Which communities do you belong to?

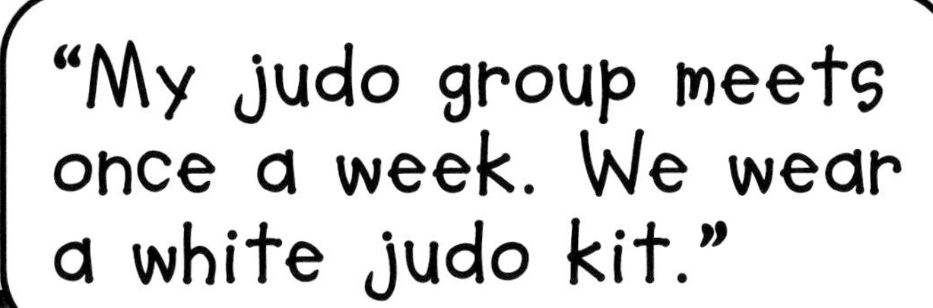

"My judo group meets once a week. We wear a white judo kit."

"I love the beautiful clothes girls and women wear in my community."

Why is it wrong to tease someone who is different from you?

What do people need?

In our diverse world, we all have the same basic needs. We all need food to eat, water to drink and somewhere to live.

◀ These children are talking about staple foods. Staple foods are things like bread or potatoes that people eat every day. Where in the world is rice a staple food?

needs staple foods

Everyone needs water. How do you get the water you need?

▶ In some places in Africa, people have to fetch their water from wells. They may only have one bucket of water a day to use for washing, cleaning, cooking and drinking. Do you think that is enough?

wells   bucket

Getting what we need

The food we eat comes from many different countries. We depend on farmers in other countries to grow many kinds of food for us. The farmers depend on the money people pay them for the food. We are interdependent.

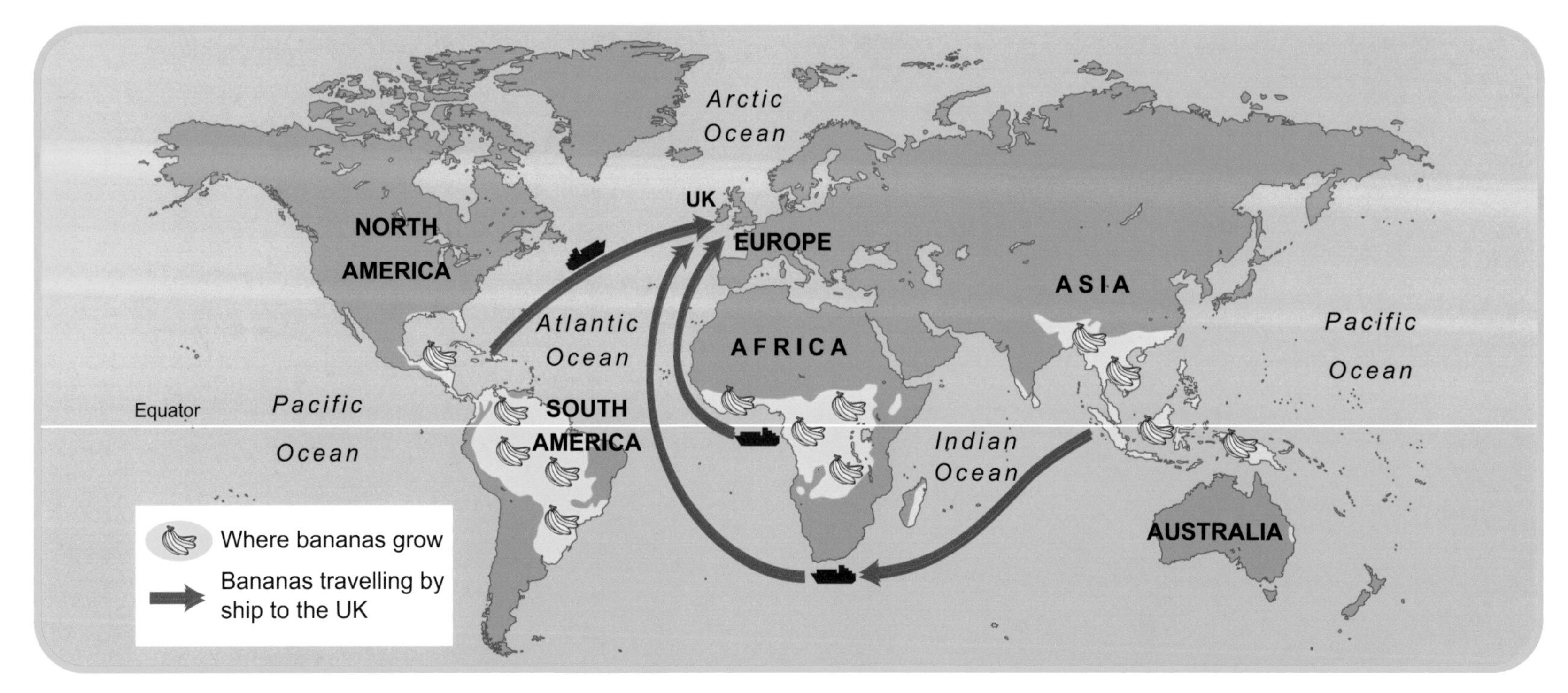

▲ Bananas only grow outside in tropical parts of the world where it is very hot. The bananas travel across the ocean to the UK in large ships.

depend interdependent tropical

◀ **Hannah is making notes about where different foods come from. She is going to put labels on a map to show how far some different foods have travelled.**

How could you find out where some of your toys and clothes are made? Can you find these places on a map?

notes travelled

Homes in different places

All the people in our diverse world need a home or somewhere to shelter. What is your home like?

► How is this home in Japan similar to your home? How is it different?

Have you stayed in a home in a different country? Has anyone in your school lived in another country? In what ways was it different?

home shelter

Homes are where we live with our family. How many people live in your home? As part of a family we have a responsibility to help around the house.

"I like having a big family. There is always someone to play with!"
"One of our jobs is to wash the car every week."

What jobs do you do to help your family?

family responsibility

Diverse religions

In our diverse world, people belong to many different religious communities. They worship in different places.

▲ Max is Christian. He enjoys singing in church on Sundays.

▲ These children are Jewish. They worship in a synagogue.

religious worship synagogue

▼ **Many Muslim children go to classes at a mosque after school to learn about their religion.**

► **Muslims say their prayers in the Arabic language. The Muslim holy book is written in Arabic.**

Muslim mosque language holy

Celebrations

In our diverse world different communities celebrate different holidays. Some of these are religious festivals. At festival time people eat special foods, sing special songs and attend services in their place of worship.

◀ Christmas is an important celebration for many people in Christian countries.

Which festivals or special days do you celebrate?

celebrate festivals services

Many communities celebrate other kinds of special days. Chinese people celebrate the start of their new year in February. They make paper decorations, share special meals, give gifts and let off fireworks.

◀ Some people make paper dragons for Chinese New Year. The dragon is a symbol of strength, goodness and good luck.

Does your family have special traditions to celebrate new year?

decorations symbol traditions

Learning and playing

In our diverse world all children have a right to an education. This means that all children should have a chance to go to school.

◀ Some school lessons are in buildings with lots of books. In this school in Nepal lessons take place outside!

In some places, children do not go to school at all. They may work instead, to help their family buy food. Do you think this is fair?

right education fair

All children also have the right to play. Children play games all over the world. What are your favourite games? Why is it important for children to play?

▲ In some places children make their own toys. These children in South Africa made their toys from recycled wire. How does using things that have been thrown away help the environment?

recycled environment

Living in a diverse world

There is a diverse mix of people living in the UK today. Some people come from other countries to find work in the UK.

◀ **In the 1950s, people were invited to come to the UK from the Caribbean. From then on, people from many countries started to come to the UK.**

invited   Caribbean

Some people come to the UK as refugees. Refugees leave their country because it is not safe. Josef is a refugee. He cannot speak English well yet. Some people at his school call him names. Why is this wrong?

▲ Josef's class decided to make some class rules about how people should treat each other. John kindly offered to be Josef's buddy and help him settle in to the school.

refugees buddy

Making connections

Becky's school has made a connection with a school in India where children learn English. The children in the two schools start to send each other emails. What would you write to someone in a school far away?

Dear Maya
My name is Becky. I live in Devon.
There are 180 children in my school. I
live with my Mum, Dad and two
brothers. We have a pet dog called
Jack. Do you have any pets?
Brenda the Bold
Freckle Juice
The Disappearing Granny
Snotty and the Rod of Power

◀ Becky describes what her school and home are like.

connection emails describes

◀ The school decides to have a special Indian week. The children research some facts about India. They read about the kinds of food people eat and the clothes people wear there.

◀ During the week the children get the chance to try on some Indian clothes.

What country would you like to learn about?

Further information for

New words listed in the text:

bucket
buddy
Caribbean
celebrate
communities
connection
decorations
depend
describes
diverse
education
emails
environment
facts
fair
family
festivals
holy
home
identity
individuals
interdependent
invited
language
mosque
Muslim
needs
notes
recycled
refugees
religious
research
responsibility
right
self-portrait
services
shelter
staple foods
symbol
synagogue
tease
traditions
travelled
tropical
wells
worship

Possible Activities

PAGES 4-5
Children could draw or make a coat of arms with a symbol on representing their own individual identity. Then to help them understand that they are also part of other groups, you could get them to form groups such as boys and girls, those with the same colour eyes or hair, or those belonging to the same club. Encourage them to think about why we should respect each other's choices, similarities and differences. Children could discuss how it feels to be teased, ensuring everyone takes turns speaking and listening appropriately.

PAGES 6-7
Children could make a poster showing foods eaten by people in different countries and the different kinds of food available in the UK. This could also be linked to work on healthy eating and making healthy choices. Children could also discuss what foods they like, which is another aspect of their identity and individuality.

PAGES 8-9
Using a world map, children could use ribbon to show their connections with other parts of world through some of the food or other products they buy or use. Encourage children to think about the ways in which people in the UK and people in other countries are interdependent. We depend on people in other countries to supply food and other products and people in those countries depend on their trade with the UK. In a circle time session, children could discuss and debate fair trade, so people who grow products for export get paid a fair wage and can afford to buy food for their own families.

PAGES 10-11
Children could collect pictures of different homes around the world (perhaps from travel magazines) and link to geography work on where these are (looking at maps) and why they are different. The children could draw a picture of their own home and add a word bank around the picture of words describing their home and how they feel about it.

Parents and Teachers

PAGES 12-13

In small groups, children could research a particular religion, using pre-selected books. Then each group could give a short report to the rest of the class. This is also a great opportunity to link with RE and invite a guest speaker in to talk about their religion. You could also organise a visit to a place of worship and encourage the children to think of questions to ask.

PAGES 14-15

There are lots of art activities that link to the study of other cultures' traditions and festivals and these are a fun way to introduce new cultures. The Oxfam Cool Planet website has links to how people in other countries live, and http://www.the-north-pole.com/around/index.htm is a useful website.

PAGES 16-17

School is an important community to which the children belong. This is a chance for them to discuss what they like and dislike about school. When talking about rights this is a good time to introduce a class vote on a topic that is of interest to them. They could also find out about some new playground games from different cultures or design and make their own toys from recycled items.

PAGES 18-19

After listening to a story about a child's experience as a refugee (such as A Friend for Farouk at http://www.citizenship foundation.org.uk/lib_res_pdf/0106.pdf) children could write their own short piece describing how they would feel if they went to a new school in a different country where they did not understand the language very well. As a class, children could also debate bullying and come up with a set of rules to prevent bullying.

Further Information

BOOKS FOR CHILDREN

A Country Far Away by Nigel Gray and Philippe Dupasquier (Orchard Books, 1991)

Homes (Around the World series) by Margaret Hall (Heinemann Library, 2003)

People and Places: Oxford First Encyclopedia by Andrew Langley (Oxford University Press, 2002)

A Faith Like Mine (Dorling Kindersley Publishers Ltd, 2005)

WEBSITES

http://www.bullying.co.uk
http://www.childline.org.uk
http://www.christian-aid.org.uk
http://www.fairtrade.org.uk
http://www.globaldimension.org.uk
http://www.globalgang.org.uk
http://www.oxfam.org.uk/coolplanet
http://www.unicef.org.uk

PAGES 20-21

Ask the children to write an email or letter describing their school or life to an imaginary (or ideally real) child in another country or another part of the UK. Encourage them to describe what the school looks like, what their uniform is like if they have one, who works or helps at the school and the different lessons and activities they do. (Guidelines on setting up a school link are available from the British Council's Education and Training Group.)

Index